Cindy Rodríguez

OHIO

EXPLORE THE U.S.A.

AV² provides enriched content that supplements and complements this book. Weigl's AV² books strive to create inspired learning and engage young minds in a total learning experience.

Your AV² Media Enhanced books come alive with...

Audio
Listen to sections of the book read aloud.

Key Words
Study vocabulary, and complete a matching word activity.

Video
Watch informative video clips.

Quizzes
Test your knowledge.

Embedded Weblinks
Gain additional information for research.

Slide Show
View images and captions, and prepare a presentation.

Try This!
Complete activities and hands-on experiments.

... and much, much more!

Go to www.av2books.com, and enter this book's unique code.

BOOK CODE

B773367

AV² by Weigl brings you media enhanced books that support active learning.

Published by AV² by Weigl
350 5th Avenue, 59th Floor
New York, NY 10118
Website: www.av2books.com   www.weigl.com

Library of Congress Cataloging-in-Publication Data
Rodriguez, Cindy.
 Ohio / Cindy Rodriguez.
     p. cm. -- (Explore the U.S.A.)
 Includes bibliographical references and index.
 ISBN 978-1-61913-389-1 (hard cover : alk. paper)
 1. Ohio--Juvenile literature. I. Title.
 F491.3.R63 2013
 977.1--dc23
                    2012015610

Printed in the United States of America in North Mankato, Minnesota
1 2 3 4 5 6 7 8 9   16 15 14 13 12

052012
WEP040512

Project Coordinator: Karen Durrie
Art Director: Terry Paulhus

Weigl acknowledges Getty Images as the primary image supplier for this title.

OHIO

Contents

3

This is Ohio.
It is called the Buckeye State.
The buckeye tree grows in Ohio.

This is the shape of Ohio. It is bordered by five other states.

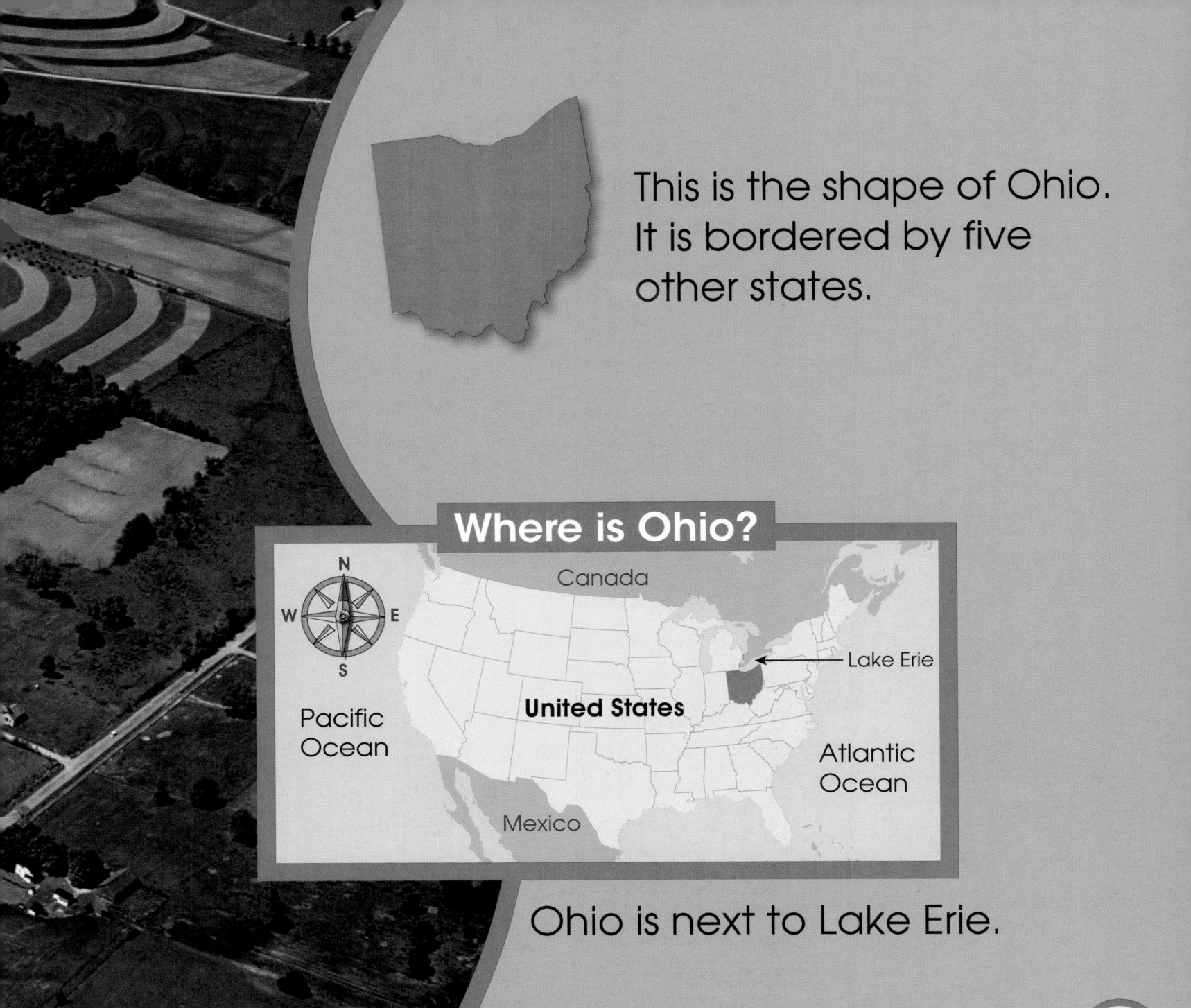

Where is Ohio?

N
W   E
S

Canada

Pacific Ocean

United States

Lake Erie

Atlantic Ocean

Mexico

Ohio is next to Lake Erie.

Beavers were important in Ohio long ago. People used beaver furs as money.

Ohio once had beavers the size of black bears.

The red carnation is the Ohio state flower. Carnations can be many different colors.

The Ohio state seal has wheat, a mountain, a river, and the Sun.

The Sun on the seal has 13 rays.

This is the state flag of Ohio.
It is red, white, and blue.
The flag has 17 white stars.

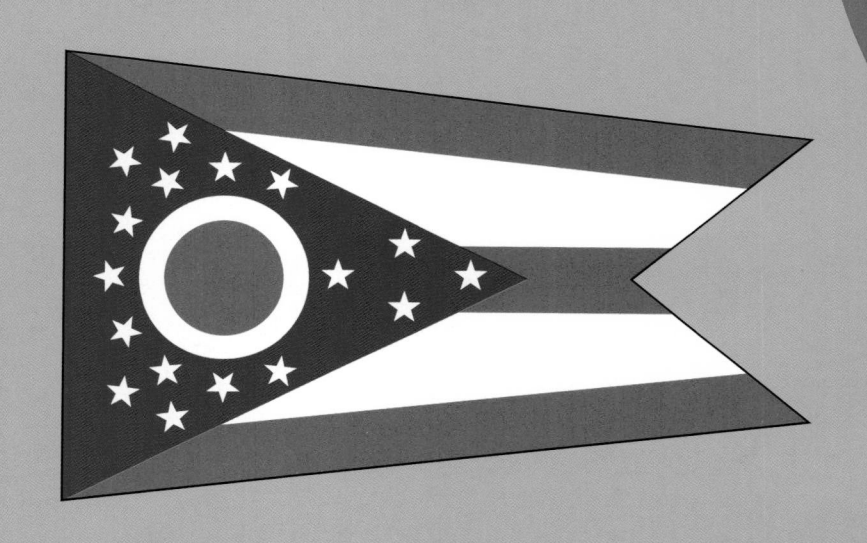

The flag also has
an O for Ohio.

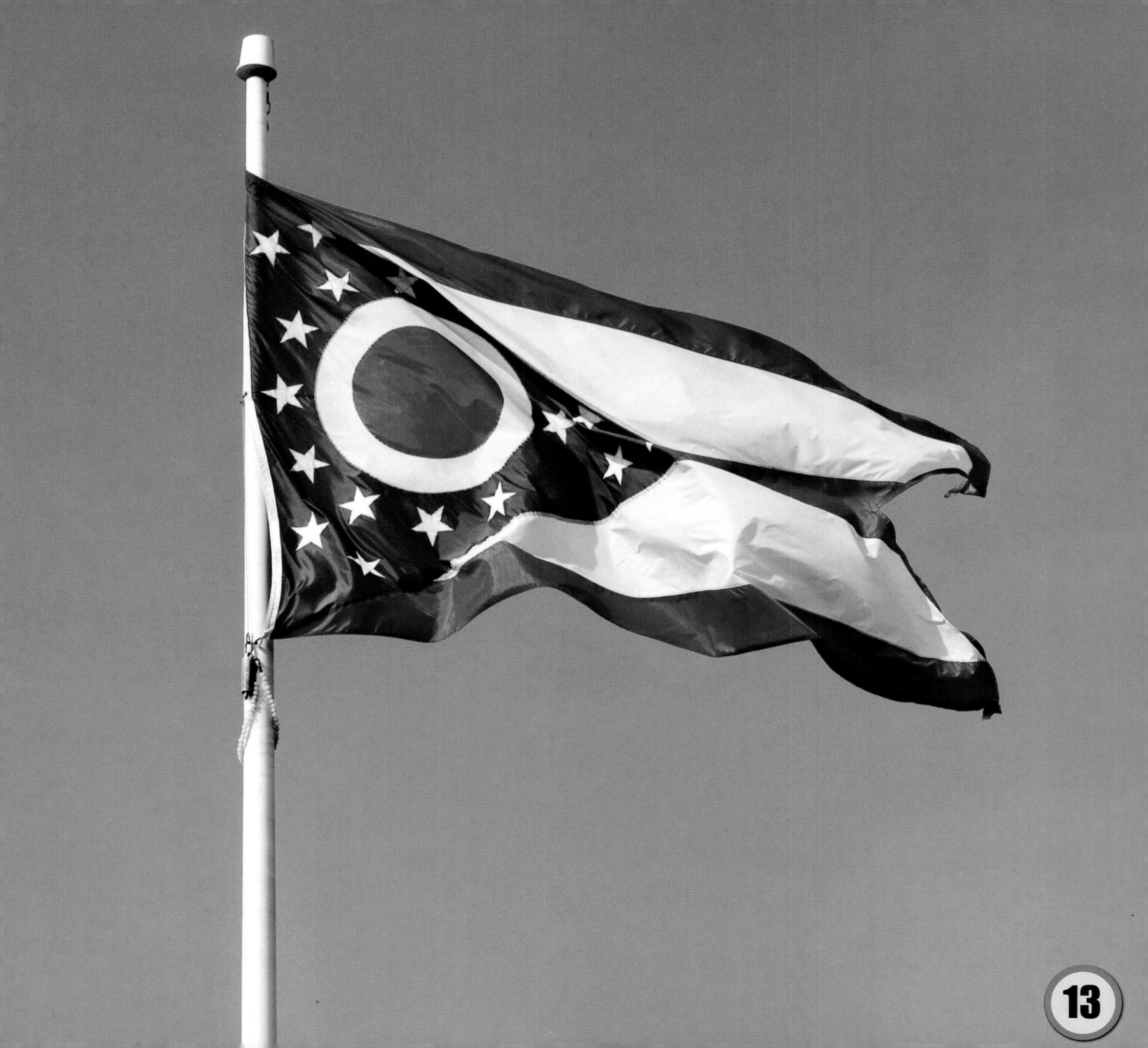

The Ohio state animal is the white-tailed deer. There are many of these deer in Ohio. A white-tailed deer baby is called a fawn.

A fawn weighs less than 4 pounds when it is born.

This is the biggest city in Ohio.
It is named Columbus.
Columbus is the state capital.

The city of Columbus
was named after
Christopher Columbus.

19

Ohio has a popcorn museum.

Corn grows in Ohio. Popcorn is a kind of corn. People in the United States eat 16 billion quarts of popcorn each year.

Ohio is known for its many lakes, rivers, and parks.

People come to Ohio to enjoy beaches, ride boats, and visit corn mazes.

OHIO FACTS

These pages provide detailed information that expands on the interesting facts found in the book. These pages are intended to be used by adults as a learning support to help young readers round out their knowledge of each state in the *Explore the U.S.A.* series.

Pages 4–5

Ohio's nickname comes from the buckeye tree that grows throughout the state. European settlers used it for building. The American Indians gave the tree its name because its nut looks like the shape and color of a deer's eye. The American Indians roasted, peeled, and mashed buckeye nuts for food.

Pages 6–7

On March 1, 1803, Ohio became the 17th state to join the United States. The Ohio River is one of the largest rivers in North America. It forms Ohio's south border with Kentucky and West Virginia. Indiana borders Ohio to the west, and Pennsylvania is to the east. Michigan and Lake Erie form Ohio's northern border.

Pages 8–9

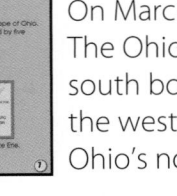

Beavers were hunted for meat and their pelts. When European settlers arrived in Ohio, American Indians began to trade pelts with them for guns and tools. For about 200 years, Europeans valued fur more than any other resource. Beaver fur was thick, warm, and water repellent. By 1830, the beaver was extinct in Ohio. More than 100 years later, beavers appeared again.

Pages 10–11

The red carnation was chosen to honor President William McKinley, who came from Ohio. He often wore a red carnation in his buttonhole. Ohio's diverse landscapes are represented on the state seal. A wheat sheaf stands by a bundle of 17 arrows, representing Ohio as the 17th state. The 13 sunrays above Mount Logan honor the original 13 colonies.

The Ohio flag was adopted in 1901. It is the only state flag that has a pennant shape. The large blue triangle represents Ohio's hills. The stripes stand for Ohio's roads and waterways. The white circle is an O for Ohio. The flag has 17 white stars to symbolize that Ohio was the 17th state.

American Indians hunted deer for food. They used the hide for clothing and the bones and antlers for tools. Deerskin hides were very valuable to early settlers. The white-tailed deer was so widely hunted that, by 1904, it was no longer found in Ohio. A restocking program and hunting regulations have since restored the deer population.

Columbus became the state capital in 1816. An 11-mile (18-kilometer) feeder canal was built in 1831. It gave the city access to the Ohio River and the Erie Canal. Before the Civil War, Columbus was an important stop on the Underground Railroad. Columbus residents helped slaves fleeing from the southern United States find a safe place to live.

Ohio is the fourth largest producer of popcorn in the United States. The Wyandot Popcorn Museum is in Marion, Ohio. The museum has antique popcorn machines and popcorn-related memorabilia. Marion hosts the largest popcorn festival in the world. More than 250,000 people attend the Marion Popcorn Festival each year.

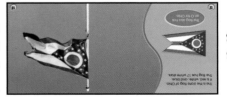

Ohio has 312 miles (502 kilometers) of shoreline on Lake Erie. Cedar Point, on the shore of Lake Erie, has a beach and an amusement park. The park features 17 rollercoasters. Corn mazes are a popular attraction in Ohio. Adventure Acres in Bellbrook has more than 11 miles (18 kilometers) of pathways through five mazes.

KEY WORDS

Research has shown that as much as 65 percent of all written material published in English is made up of 300 words. These 300 words cannot be taught using pictures or learned by sounding them out. They must be recognized by sight. This book contains 52 common sight words to help young readers improve their reading fluency and comprehension. This book also teaches young readers several important content words, such as proper nouns. These words are paired with pictures to aid in learning and improve understanding.

Page	Sight Words First Appearance
4	grows, in, is, it, state, the, this, tree
7	by, next, of, other, to, where
8	as, had, important, long, once, people, used, were
11	a, and, be, can, different, has, many, mountain, on, river
12	also, an, for, white
15	animal, are, than, there, these, when
16	after, city, named, was
19	each, eat, kind, year
20	come, its

Page	Content Words First Appearance
4	buckeye, Ohio
7	Lake Erie, shape
8	beavers, black bears, furs, money, size
11	carnation, colors, flower, rays, seal, Sun, wheat
12	flag, stars
15	baby, fawn, pounds, white-tailed deer
16	capital, Christopher Columbus, Columbus
19	corn, museum, popcorn, quarts, United States
20	beaches, boats, lakes, mazes, parks

24